Thor Heyerdahl and the Reed Boat *Ra*

BARBARA BEASLEY MURPHY and **NORMAN BAKER, Navigator**

Foreword by Thor Heyerdahl

J. B. LIPPINCOTT COMPANY

PHILADELPHIA AND NEW YORK

FOR JENNIFER AND STEPHEN MURPHY

AND

FOR DANIEL, ELIZABETH, AND MITCHELL BAKER

U.S. Library of Congress Cataloging in Publication Data

Murphy, Barbara.
  Thor Heyerdahl and the reed boat Ra.

  SUMMARY: Describes the events of the two Atlantic crossings made by Thor
Heyerdahl and an international crew in papyrus boats, replicas of those used by
the ancient Egyptians.
  1. Ra (Boat)—Juvenile literature. 2. Voyages and travels—1951- —Juvenile
literature. [1. Ra (Boat) 2. Voyages and travels] I. Baker, Norman Kent, birth
date joint author. II. Title.
G530.M98   910.09′163   73-20260
ISBN-0-397-31503-1

Foreword

Norman Baker is the American who sailed with me in a boat of reeds across the Atlantic Ocean. In this book he wants to share our great adventures with you.

If you feel you have been with us when you close the pages of this book, then you have learned what we found out:

Men are like big boys; they can have more fun and get much further by sticking together in friendship than by opposing each other with guns.

Thor Heyerdahl

THOR HEYERDAHL

Thor Heyerdahl, famous for sailing the Pacific Ocean in a raft called *Kon-Tiki*, had a new idea. He suspected that people from North Africa might have crossed the Atlantic Ocean to America thousands of years before Columbus or the Vikings.

Thor, an explorer and scientist from Norway, has spent his life seeking to understand what happened in the world before people left written records. Now Thor wanted to know if it was possible that men from the oldest nations around the Holy Land, like Phoenicia and Egypt, could have made such a voyage three thousand or more years ago. He decided to find out by having a boat built like the ones ancient Egyptians had used. He planned to sail it himself across the ocean.

Many people who heard of this idea told him no one could have crossed the Atlantic Ocean before waterproof wooden boats came into use. "Those Egyptians had only reed boats for river trips. No one could sail an ocean in one of those. The reeds would dissolve in two weeks! You'd be dumped in the sea! It's ridiculous!"

Thor's studies in the years before 1969 made him suspect that the Egyptians or their neighbors could have reached America and shared their great ideas and knowledge with some of the Indians there. The Aztec, Maya, and Inca nations seemed to reveal a connection between these distant parts of the ancient world.

The nations of Phoenicia and Egypt were known to have sent their best-educated men on voyages. Like the ancient captains, Thor wanted a crew of intelligent and brave men. He needed a navigator learned in the ways of the sea who could read the stars at night to keep the boat on course. He imagined the explorers of long ago bringing a doctor to guard their health and their wisest priest to pray for Ra's blessing. Ra was the sun god they worshiped. Thor would need a doctor, too, and a deep-sea diver to make underwater repairs on the boat. He'd bring a photographer, so that when the voyage was ended there would be pictures to prove it had been done.

Thor began to search for men who, like himself, were eager to make such a voyage. He thought it would be a good experiment to invite someone from the United States and someone from Russia, someone who was black and others who weren't. He thought an Arab could get along with a Jew on such a trip, a Christian with a Muslim. He felt the crew would show the world they could work together even though they were of different races, nations, and religions. And while doing so, they would help him to prove that people could have reached America from North Africa long before anyone so far had thought possible.

NORMAN BAKER

Thor had to travel widely to prepare for this voyage. In the United States he looked up Norman Baker, whom he had met years before on the island of Tahiti. Norman, an engineer, is a Commander in the Naval Reserve. He had sailed the South Seas and climbed the Matterhorn. He was known to his friends as a man with great courage and persistence. Thor admired his spirit and enjoyed his sense of humor. He seemed to be the ideal navigator for the boat.

When Thor met with Norman, he told him that there were signs of ancient Middle East life in ancient Indian life. Norman was fascinated. Thor told him that people in both areas wrote in hieroglyphs or pictures. Their calendars were similar. Scientists had found human skulls, several thousand years old, which showed that the same kind of brain operation was performed by the Indians and the Egyptians. Like the Egyptians, the Indians built and sailed reed boats. Reed was a strange choice in America, where wood was easily available. Thor guessed that the Indians had copied the reed boats that had come from the other side of the Atlantic. And both peoples had worshiped the sun god and built great pyramids to him. These massive wonders are found in Egypt, Mexico, and Peru.

Norman was impressed by the great explorer and all the things he told him. He, too, began to want to know if a reed boat could have crossed the ocean. When Thor finally asked him to come along as his navigator, Norman and his wife agreed that he should go.

Thor made further preparations. He studied records left by the ancient Egyptians. In museums he saw models and pictures of reed boats. In one he discovered something that made him more certain that the boats had been used on the ocean as well as on rivers. A fish was pictured in the water beneath a boat. Thor recognized it as an ocean fish, a kind never found in rivers or lakes.

Thor went to see the reed boats still being used in South America, on Lake Titicaca in Bolivia. He also found some in Mexico. On the other side of the Atlantic, he drove across the

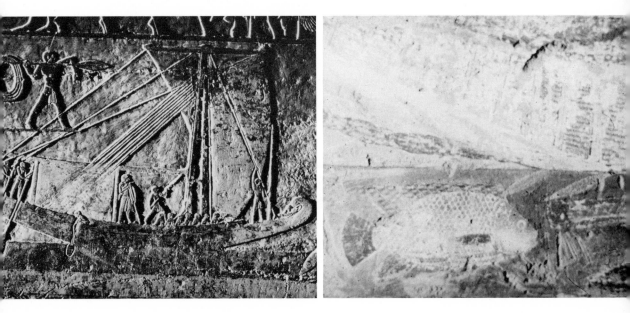

baking African desert to Lake Chad. The Buduma tribesmen of Chad still use reed boats to cross the huge lake. He found boat builders among them who said they would come to Egypt and build a boat for him. He was grateful to these brave men who would leave their homes, cone-shaped huts where they lived in the same way their ancestors had lived for hundreds of years, and go to a place that would be a new world for them.

The reeds used by the ancient Egyptians in boat building were called *papyrus*. It was from papyrus that paper, too, was first made. But papyrus was no longer grown in Egypt. The closest place where Thor could find the graceful reed was Ethiopia. He visited some black monks in the mountains of

Ethiopia and persuaded them to sell him twelve tons of papyrus. It was then shipped by truck and boat to Egypt.

Thor set up a work camp in the desert before the Great Pyramids. The Buduma boat builders soaked the papyrus reeds in drums of water. Then they bound the softened papyrus into bundles, lashing the reeds together with ropes. The bundles were formed into a boat fifty feet long and sixteen feet wide. The design of the boat followed the ancient models

and pictures Thor had seen. Like the ancient boats, Thor's was made entirely of reeds and ropes, with a cabin of wicker lashed to wooden cross beams. Not a single nail or screw was used in the construction.

In the dry air of the desert, under the blistering sun, the men worked. Thor worried that a spark from a cigarette or a fire would accidentally send his dream up in smoke.

ABDULLAH DJIBRIME

By now he had rounded up his crew from all parts of the world. One of the tribesmen who spoke French, Abdullah Djibrime, wanted to go along on the boat he was helping to build. Thor agreed. It would be good to have a crewman who was skilled at making repairs on the boat.

People continued to make fun of Thor's plans, even when they saw the boat nearly finished. Some of them presented strong arguments against the idea of the voyage. Finally someone sneered, "You can't sail the ocean in a *paper* boat!"

Their objections might have stopped many thoughtful men. The urge to try it, however, was really part of Thor. He listened with kind attention to all the questions. But in his head he went right on sailing to America in a papyrus reed boat.

By April of 1969 the boat called *Ra*, in honor of the Egyptian sun god, was completed. The government of Egypt, in celebration, sent five hundred athletes to pull the boat across the desert on log rollers. Then the boat was carried by truck to the port of Safi, Morocco, on the northwest coast of Africa.

It took another month to set the mast, rig the sails, build the rudders, and set up the cabin for sleeping and the open galley for cooking. The crew stored food and all the equipment they might need for sailing, navigating, treating illness, and making repairs.

When *Ra* was launched, she floated like a cork. In time she settled deeper in the waters of the harbor. The reeds began to swell as they absorbed the salt water. Someone had told Thor his boat would sink within two weeks. After one week *Ra* was lower in the water, but the captain of the boat never thought she would sink.

On the last day in Safi, the flags from the countries of the crewmen were strung up on *Ra:* Chad, Egypt, Italy, Mexico, Norway, the Soviet Union, and the United States. Thor also flew the flag of the United Nations as a symbol of unity.

With her flags flying, *Ra* put to sea May 27, 1969. A huge sun glowed on her deep red sail. The shore was lined with hundreds of people: well-wishers, relatives, doubters, and newsmen. They watched the golden, basketlike *Ra* sail like a paper swan out of the harbor. They watched until she could be seen no more.

Ra was on her way across the ocean with her crew of seven men. They sailed on the current that always moves westward. The trade winds from the coast of Africa filled the sails and helped push her toward America. The boat creaked and groaned like a monster, snaking through the sea.

On board, Norman and some of the others worked on the problems of sailing *Ra*. There had not been time to try her out before leaving. The time of bad storms on the Atlantic would come in July, and they had to try to get to America before that. Thor expected the voyage to take less than two months.

The huge sail caught the wind, and they were moving well, but the rudders for steering seemed very difficult to work. They looked like two long oars that slanted down from the steering platform into the sea. Thor found it took great strength to control them.

Ra was packed full. The men had to walk around and over things. The cabin was eight by twelve feet, the size of a small bedroom. Their mattresses were laid on top of packing cases. Three slept in one row and four in another. As the boat tilted on the sea, the sleeping men would slide down on top of one another until the one on the bottom cried out!

Georges Sourial and Santiago Genoves set up the galley for cooking. Georges, a deep-sea diver from Egypt, is an exuberant storyteller, who never leaves any place without making friends. He and Santiago, a professor from Mexico, were amazed and amused at some of the strange foods they were storing. There were no canned goods. They would eat the very same kinds of food that the ancient sailors had eaten: fresh meat from live chickens, smoked meats, hard breads, dried fruits, and nuts. Most of the food was stored in earthenware jars lashed securely to the boat. Eggs were packed in

lime. Five hundred gallons of drinking water were stored in jars and goatskin bags. (The water in those bags tasted like goats! It was the ancient way.) There were cheeses, tea and coffee, salt and spices. The sea gave them pompano, dolphin, and flying fish. For quick snacks there was a nourishing mixture of grain, dates, and honey.

Some of the pictures of ancient boats had shown monkeys on board. To complete the unusual crew, the Pasha of Safi had presented Thor with a little gray one. She was named Safi after the port. Safi found *Ra* a wonderful playground. She swung from ropes and sail, crawled over the cabin, and busied herself with the pans in the galley. She kept the crewmen chasing after her, cleaning up the messes she made from one end of the boat to the other. Georges became one of the first heroes of the voyage by managing to get Safi into diapers. That made everyone's life easier!

The men were convinced that the papyrus was seaworthy, but they were having a devilish time handling the boat. On the first day out the rudder oars had broken. Thor realized too late that they had not been made thick enough to stand the force of the rough ocean waves. There was no way to turn the boat around and go back. It could only go in the direction the wind and water drove it. With the help of others, Abdullah the boat builder and Thor worked to repair the rudders. They strengthened them with extra wood they had brought along. They worked through the day and into the night, not resting, until the winds subsided and the boat was in fair control.

Suddenly Norman, the only experienced sailor, came down with a tropical fever. Yuri Senkevitch, the doctor from Russia, gave him antibiotics and put him to bed. In ancient times a sick sailor might have died. Norman lay tossing in the creaking cabin, while all the excitement of the voyage went on around him. The reeds creaked and groaned, making it hard for him to sleep.

The next day the yardarm spreading the sail in the wind cracked and fell. The wind increased and pulled the lines out of the men's hands as they struggled to control *Ra*. Waves were flung across the deck. The boat was tossed like a castaway basket on the sea. Thor cried out orders first in one language and then another. Somehow each man was able to understand.

YURI SENKEVITCH

The clay jars of food that were lashed to the deck of the boat began to bang against one another. Some of them cracked and the contents came spilling out. Men rushed around, trying to rescue the food from the broken jars and to make the others secure. Safi also rushed around. She was quick to find the broken jars and gobbled up the nuts and dates that had miraculously appeared.

Each man took his turn at the heavy rudder oars. They were somewhat alarmed at the great damage to the boat so early in the voyage. But despite all the difficulties *Ra* continued on course. Norman, well again, charted about seventy miles each day.

The papyrus took to the salt water. No longer brittle and fragile, the wet reeds had become supple and strong. Day by

day they became less likely to burn from an accidental spark. As they soaked up water, the reeds swelled and became as tough and resilient as automobile tires. When they were squeezed, air bubbled out. Thor realized that seawater washing in and out prevented them from souring and dissolving.

In the beginning the men took turns preparing meals and cleaning up. At first Georges, who had been brought up in a household where servants did all the chores, left his clothes and possessions wherever he happened to drop them. The other men finally complained to Thor, who spoke to Georges about it. Georges took Thor's advice to heart and tried to reform. Hoping to make amends, he took charge of cleaning the galley after meals. Everyone was grateful and pleased.

Most of the problems that arose on board were dealt with in a democratic way. Each man's opinion and feelings were respected and considered. Thor reserved for himself, as captain, the right of decision in the case of danger to the life of any man. He treated the men with warm affection, worrying when they were sick or upset, reminding this one to wear his hat in the sun and that one to rest. He spoke to them gently and kindly but gave firm orders when necessary.

Each man was responsible for one special part of the work. The boat, the crew, and all the details of the journey were photographed by Carlo Mauri, an Italian newspaperman who was also a famous mountain climber. He had been on many expeditions and worked hard at making a success of these adventures. Carlo took nearly all the pictures of the voyage. The underwater photographs were taken by Georges, the diver.

The man in charge of supplies was Dr. Santiago Genoves from Mexico. He is a professor who has studied ways of working out solutions among groups or nations that disagreed. Pope John XXIII's Peace Prize had been awarded to him in 1969 for his work. Thor had asked Santiago to observe and record how a crew with different customs and abilities settled problems that arose among them. Thor and Santiago believed that the crew of *Ra* could be an example that would promote brotherhood and cooperation. Like Abdullah, Santiago had never before been to sea.

CARLO MAURI

DR. SANTIAGO GENOVES

Since the boat could only follow the strong current that sent it westward, Thor was concerned that someone might fall overboard or swim out too far. If anyone did, *Ra* could not be turned around to pick him up. Thor insisted that the men tie themselves to different parts of the boat as they moved around on deck. When they swam or bathed, they tied themselves to the boat. Sometimes they tried out ancient-style life preservers made of papyrus. They were easy to get into and buoyant.

GEORGES SOURIAL

Flocks of chickens and one duck were nestled in cages. The men cooked the chickens but not the duck, whose personality was so outstanding that he became a pet. The crew called him Sinbad the Sailor, though he made it clear that he didn't like the ocean. Perhaps the sea was too rough and salty for him. He would want back in the boat almost as soon as he left it. When he did take to water, he, like everyone else, had to be tied to the boat.

A member of the crew who shared Sinbad's dislike of the salt water surrounding them was Abdullah, the boat builder. He is a Muslim, and every morning and night he must kneel and pray to Allah. Even on board *Ra* no storm or disaster stopped him. Part of his worship involved washing himself in pure water before his prayers. Abdullah had never been to the ocean, and no one had thought to tell him it was salt. He was horrified when he discovered this and felt that using ocean water was not respectful to Allah. Could he, he wondered, use some of the drinking water stored in the bags and jars? The men talked this problem over, and Abdullah realized that there was only enough water for drinking, so he decided to continue his worship with the seawater.

Most of the men followed the custom of explorers and began to let their beards and hair grow. They wanted to record how long the voyage was by how long their hair got. Yuri, the Russian doctor, however, shaved almost every day. He dressed like a yachtsman on a cruise. Abdullah laughed as the others' faces disappeared behind beards. He himself had no beard, but he let the hair on his head, which he always shaved, grow in.

Abdullah saw the other men keeping diaries of their adventures and reading books for relaxation. He asked Georges to teach him to read. Before the voyage was over, he had learned to read and write Arabic.

Each day Norman measured the height of the sun, and at night a star, with his sextant. Noting the exact time, he calculated *Ra*'s position on the sea. He drew each new position on his chart. Everyone could see where they were. Every few days Norman made a report over the radio of their position and the condition of boat and men.

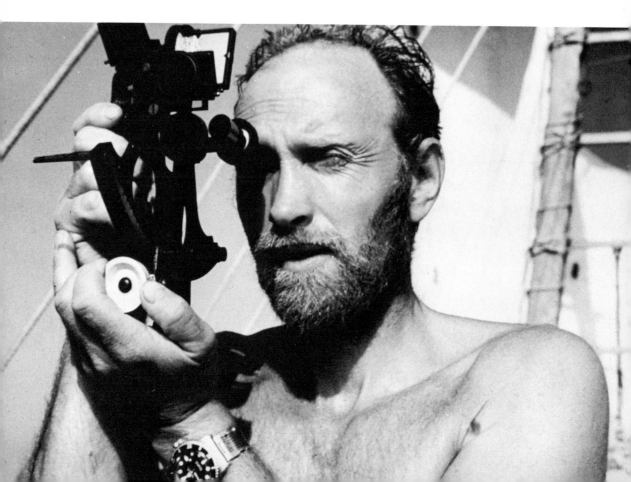

Newsmen from all over the world followed reports of the voyage carefully. One day newspapers told their readers that the stern, or back end, of the boat was not holding up.

When *Ra* was being built, there was a rope from the top of the stern down to the deck, because Thor had noticed that such a rope was in all the ancient pictures of reed boats. The builders kept tripping on it and finally cut it away. They didn't think it was needed anyway.

It was true that boats on a calm lake would not need it, but it became clear that the rope had an important purpose on a rough ocean voyage. It held the stern in a high and firm position. Without it, *Ra*'s high tail began to droop. Each day it sank lower in the water, until finally the men were able to do their laundry in the pool that formed there.

Storms came and beat at the boat, pushing the stern lower and lower. The boat seemed smaller and more cramped. Sleeping became difficult. Tempers burst and angry words were spoken. Some of the men were very industrious and serious; others were lighter-hearted and did not look for extra work. Each group sometimes resented the other. Thor, the kind listener, heard their complaints and reassured them. He told them that all kinds of people were needed for an expedition: those who carried more of the work and those who could make everyone laugh and be happy.

By the middle of June they were far into the Atlantic. The stern was getting worse. The cabin of the boat was taking a pounding because of the damaged stern. The crew worried that they might not make the thousand miles still ahead of them.

Someone looked at the plastic foam life raft. Perhaps it could be cut up and attached to the stern to help it stay afloat.

"But what about a lifeboat in case of emergency?" asked Thor.

"The papyrus floats. I'd grab a hunk of that!" replied Carlo.

"I'd never abandon the *Ra!*" insisted Yuri, who had once endured cruel cold and months of darkness in the Antarctic on an earlier expedition.

Norman smiled, feeling much the same way.

Everyone then agreed that the success of the voyage was important and that using the life raft to repair the stern was their only chance. They cut it up and tied the pieces to the stern.

It helped for a while. But day by day the stern sank deeper in the sea. Waves beat the sides of the boat and leaped over them, washing the deck with water up to the men's knees. Some of the boxes in the cabin began to break from the force. Men had to sleep outside. The stern trailed off as if it wanted to escape. Thor shook his head. "From the front *Ra* looks like a swan," he said. "But from the back she looks like a toad!"

One day sharks began to circle the boat. Brave Georges speared one to death, but more of them came. Thor felt it

was too dangerous to permit Georges to do any more under-water repair work. The ocean washed over the sides of the boat, salting the men's legs and lapping their ankles. The sharks circled patiently, hungry for a feast.

Ra was only five hundred miles from Barbados, an island near South America, when Thor decided they could safely go no farther. In fifty-six days the boat had gone nearly three thousand miles. The sail was down, and the mast leaned out toward the sea. They could make no more repairs. A small

yacht had come out with cameramen to film their last days before arrival. After sailing on for a couple more days with the yacht alongside, Thor decided to abandon *Ra*.

The men were disappointed. Some wanted to stay on and keep trying. But Thor knew it wasn't safe. A mistake had been made in the design of the boat. The men had had to learn on the voyage how to sail her. The ancient sailors would have known these things. But the voyage of *Ra* had proved that papyrus was up to ocean travel. It certainly showed that such a voyage was possible.

Finally, two months after they set out, the men loaded their possessions and pets on the rescue ship and abandoned *Ra* to the sea. Loose papyrus reeds kept drifting with the never-ending ocean currents, until four years later some were washed up on the coast of Norway, making the people there wonder.

Safi went home with Thor to be cared for by his daughters, and Sinbad went to the United States to live with Norman's children.

Thor's dream did not fade. Nor did it fade in the minds of those he had shared it with. *Ra* had sailed so far across the ocean that no one could say that it would have been impossible for ancient man to have completed such a voyage. Still Thor wasn't satisfied. Neither were the others. They wanted to try again!

This time Thor knew what the boat needed. He thought the Aymara Indians of Lake Titicaca, Bolivia, could build him a stronger boat, because they used a different method of working with reeds. Thor persuaded four of these Indians to fly with their interpreter to Morocco, where they built a much tighter boat out of long bundles of papyrus reeds. The stern was tied securely, and the rudder oars were thick tree trunks.

The Indians became homesick and wanted to finish quickly so they could return to South America. They used only nine of the twelve tons of papyrus available, and *Ra II* ended up shorter than the first boat by nearly ten feet.

All the crewmen joined Thor again in Safi. Abdullah, however, left for home just before *Ra II* sailed when his new wife gave birth to a child. Thor had signed on two new crew members, Madani Ait Ouhanni from Morocco and Kei Ohara from Japan. Safi and Sinbad were there, too.

Flying only one flag, that of the United Nations, *Ra II*, with a crew of eight men, was launched at Safi on May 17, 1970. She perched high in the sea, taut and ready to fly. The first *Ra* had relaxed in the water, undulating like a snake. *Ra II* was a powerful headstrong bird.

Her first day out, the wind carried her ninety-five miles down the coast of Africa, racing toward dangerous Cape Sim. Sea-hidden rocks had caused many ships to be dashed to pieces there over thousands of years. The crew fought to control the sail and rudders. They yelled and pulled at the boat's lines. The more they struggled to control her, the more she struggled free.

In a half-gale wind she sailed under soaring white clouds.

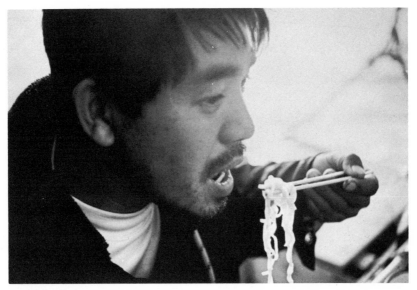

KEI OHARA

The sky was dark. The moon flashed in and out of the clouds. The warning lighthouses were blinking. The rocks were only yards away.

Then a line snapped, and the bottom of the great red sail whipped loose. The flailing yardarm, to which the canvas was attached, nearly tore the mast and rigging down.

The crew fought to furl the sail. The wind and sea fought to tear it away. Finally it was furled, and the boat slowed. Norman flung up a small sail, which the wind pinned against the mast, and *Ra II* gracefully avoided the rocks. Miraculously tamed, she floated through the night. One man stood watch, two were seasick, and the rest of the exhausted crew slept.

On the second day of the voyage of *Ra II* the crew repaired the sail and put the deck in order. On the third day they were sailing again. Norman, who was second in command, began sending radio bulletins to keep the world advised of their progress. Thor began a log of his second journey in a reed boat. Santiago, Yuri, and Georges arranged the supplies and set up the galley and cabin.

MADANI AIT OUHANNI

Carlo had asked for someone to help with the filming. The new crewman Kei was an expedition photographer and would join Carlo in the work.

On the first trip the crew had been shocked by all the filth floating in the water. Sometimes they could not brush their teeth in it because of oil clots, slime, or other pollution. The other new crew member, Madani, took the daily task of collecting samples of the pollution, so that the sad condition of our sea could be brought to the attention of the world. Into Madani's net fell black wads of oil, bottles, plastic in all shapes, and aerosol cans. The men who had been on the previous voyage found that the condition of the sea seemed worse after only one year.

Sinbad the duck strutted around, munching seed and grain and trying to avoid the water. Safi explored the new boat, playing happily.

Several land birds that had flown too far from home fluttered down from the sky. There was one sick pigeon who wouldn't eat. Georges took pity on the bird. He chewed up food and fed the weak bird from his own mouth until it recovered.

On the fourth day the sea was calm and the sky serene. At first the men were glad to have time for rest and talking, but the calm continued for many days. After a while the days seemed long and dull, and the crew grew restless and uneasy. *Ra II,* though small, was a heavy boat and had soaked up gallons of water in her reeds. She settled deeper into the sea, and Thor worried that the added weight would slow her down when the wind finally did pick up.

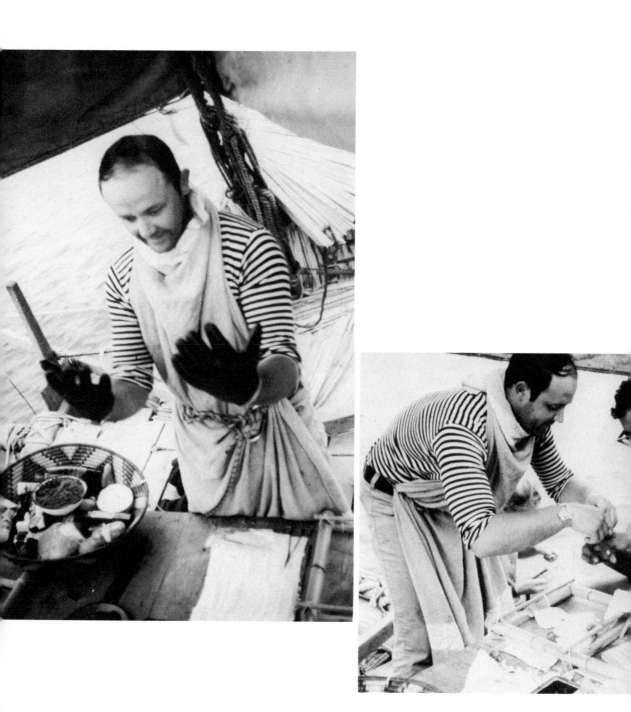

One day Georges' finger became so inflamed from an injury that he showed it to Yuri. The doctor worried that the infection would become worse if he did not work on it immediately. The announcement of the operation was big news on the little boat. Everyone wanted to help. Santiago dressed up as a nurse and the others put on serious faces. They gathered around to watch while Yuri cut open Georges' finger and cleaned out the infection. There was no medicine to numb the finger. Georges bore the operation as long as he could and then yelled at Yuri, telling him he was a terrible doctor and that no one in Egypt would have caused him such pain. Yuri laughed and told him that no one in Russia would have cried over such a little thing!

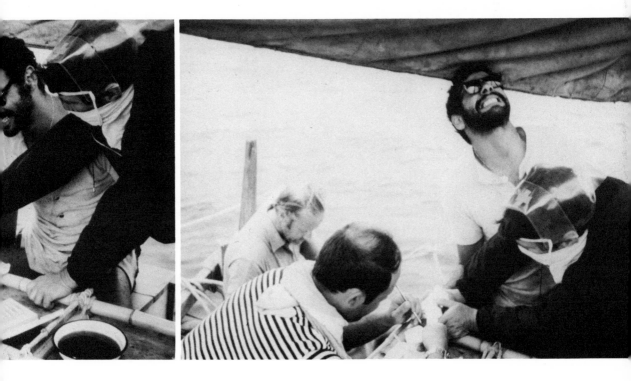

After a week the trade winds returned, filling the sails and pushing *Ra II* west, in the path of the sun. She was none the slower for her rest. Norman plotted eighty-one miles in a single day. But the boat seemed dangerously low in the water, so the crew threw overboard anything heavy that wasn't absolutely necessary. Into the sea went a large tree trunk that could have made an extra rudder oar, clay jars of food, and even some drinking water.

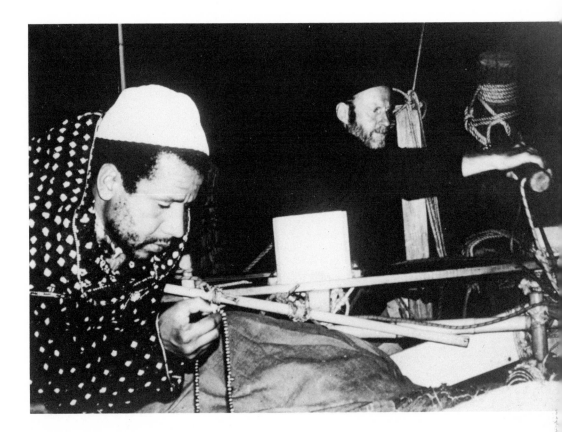

Each man took his turn steering with the heavy rudders. It was hard work. In the evening Madani, a Muslim, faced Mecca and prayed. During the nights they took turns at keeping watch. There were always sails and lines to mend. The crew found time for entertainment, too. They taught each other words from their native languages and filled their diaries with events of the voyage and stories of their companions. Norman played his harmonica, Santiago and Georges danced, and all the men talked of their families at home.

At the end of the thirty-second day they had traveled over halfway, eighteen hundred miles. There were fifteen hundred more to go.

The crew celebrated this good news by having a party. Georges made an astonishing dinner from the meager supplies. Fresh fish, cheese, and artichokes in olive oil were put out on the table. Toasts were drunk with Italian wine, Russian vodka, and American champagne! Safi chattered and Sinbad quacked. The crew sang and joked far into the night.

The next day, June 18, 1970, *Ra II* was moving fast in the strong wind and the sunlight. Carlo was fishing from the bow. Suddenly a valley of sea opened in front of the boat. As Carlo scrambled back from the edge, *Ra II* was carried up the watery mountain. This kind of wave, a freak known to sailors as an augmented wave, is two waves that catch up with each other and build to a crest twice as high as either would have made alone.

The boat rose up and slid over the crest. Moments later a second valley seemed to swallow her. And again she started up a mountainlike wave of extraordinary height. Norman, in the cabin, felt the rushing ascent and stopped working on his chart.

Just as the second crest caught up with *Ra II*, the wave broke. *Ra II* plummeted down the waterfall. Thor, steering, watched in horror as the boat raced down the steep wave like a man on a surfboard. Then came the blow! There was an awful, hollow, muffled noise when she hit the bottom of the watery trough.

"Boys! All hands on deck! The rudder broke!" cried Thor.

Ra II swerved sideways toward the waves that crashed upon her. She was out of control, and the huge waves came plunging down on boat and crew. The men were scared.

They rushed to put out sea anchors to steady the boat. The sail had to be turned to catch the wind, which would otherwise blow the boat over. It took six crewmen to haul the heavy rudder, its shaft as thick as a telephone pole, aboard. They looked in horror at the stump of the rudder shaft that was still lashed to the rudder blade. There was not enough wood left on board to replace something so large.

Waves thundered over the sides of the boat. In the stern, water was up to the men's hips. With the sea anchors dragging, the stern held into the wind, and the boat rode mournfully along like a crippled bird. "If the sea can do this to us," worried Norman aloud, "what's next?"

At dawn Thor cut scale models of the broken rudder from a cardboard box. Using these, the men discussed methods of repair, fitting the pieces together in different ways to determine the best way to mend the damage. Finally they were in agreement. Thor chiseled the longest section of the broken shaft to hold the blade. It took the whole crew to lash it in place.

By sunset the work was finished. The men were amazed at their success. They had done a major repair job without modern materials or equipment, using methods the ancient Egyptians could well have used. The steering oars were workable again, but they were even more difficult to handle than before. Some of the smaller men could hardly manage the task, because it required working the shorter repaired rudder with a foot and stretching to reach the other one with the hands.

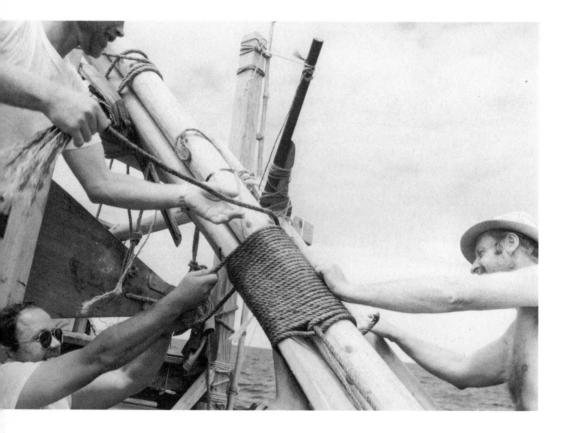

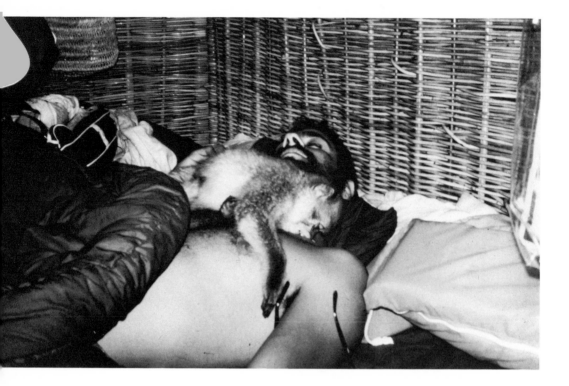

Safi, wet and nervous from the events of the past few days,
bit Kei's arm. Then in remorse she cried to be hugged. Giving
in to her, Kei was caressed by the monkey, then bitten again!
But by nightfall Safi was herself again and slept with Georges
like a baby.

The endless ocean stretched before the men as far as the
eye could see. Sometimes it seemed to hold them like a
prison. At other times they were awed by its beauty. Their
sea, their sky, their life together made their differences of
personality, nation, race, and religion seem small and insig-
nificant. They shared the common bond of being human and
having to confront the demands of their situation with human
strengths and weaknesses.

They yearned toward shore and home. Each man had his own memories to dream on. Thor remembered his home in the mountains by the sea and thought about his lovely wife Yvonne and their three blond daughters. Norman recalled a day on the beach when his wife Mary Ann and their children flew kites together. He closed his eyes against the sea and sky and imagined being with them.

The men were short of drinking water. Some of their supply had spoiled in poorly sealed bags. Some jars had broken, and some had been thrown overboard when they were trying to make the boat lighter. Thirst became a constant hardship. Each man was permitted to fill his canteen only once every second day. They began using seawater for making soup.

Everyone would have welcomed fresh fruit and vegetables. But the hot meal they had every day was a comfort to them. Flying fish landed on board, and the men ran around scooping up fresh food for their stew pot. The bread they had brought along had become as hard as rocks. They had to soak it in their soup to eat it.

The men became irritable. The boat was low in the water and they were always wet. Some got saltwater sores. Some suspected others of taking more than their share of drinking water. Feelings were hurt, manners forgotten. Thor struggled to keep peace among the men, who sometimes felt so discouraged that they would dream of rescue. A few had terrible nightmares. Yuri was hitting himself in his sleep. Norman ran on deck one night, having dreamed the mainsail was destroyed.

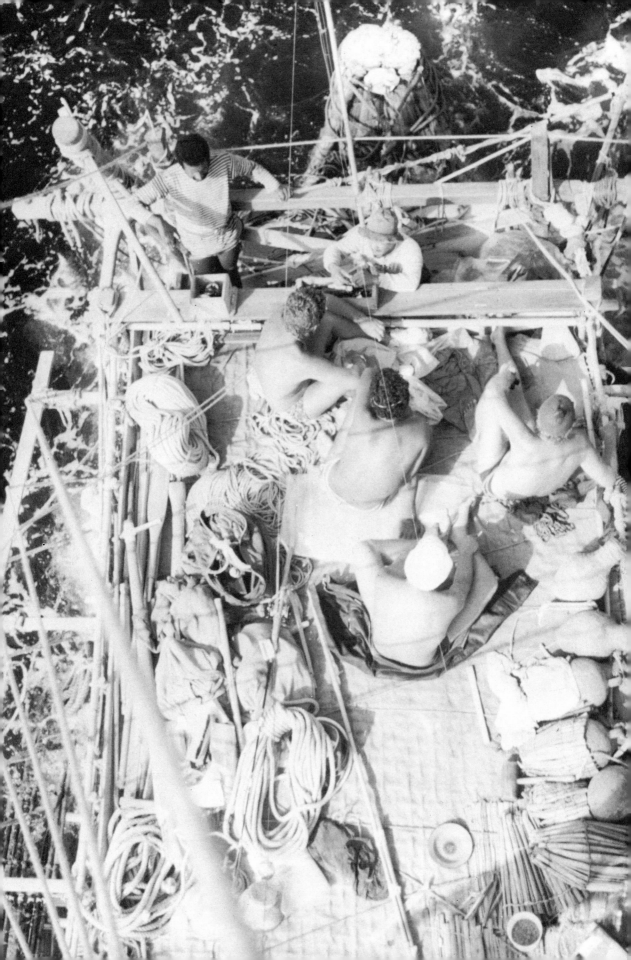

By June 27, *Ra II* had gone 2,360 miles. The crew estimated there were two more weeks of sailing ahead of them. Much of the food was gone. Repairs had used up all their supplies of rope and canvas. The men cut up their mattress covers for material to mend the sails.

Lower than ever in the water, the boat required exhausting effort to control. On the night of July 3, a storm sent waves bursting over the sides of the boat, filling the stern like a bathtub. Discouraging as that was, it was a sight of magical beauty. The water glowed with the phosphorescence of floating plankton. The boat and sea were decorated with tiny luminous plants and animals. "In spite of these mean storms," Carlo remarked, "I think the ocean is wishing us good luck."

At dawn the next day Norman noticed their pigeon circling high above the mast. Then he saw it flying on ahead. Later Yuri searched for it. It was nowhere to be found. The men wondered if it had sensed the land, still two hundred miles ahead. They worried that it might not have the strength to fly there.

Slower and slower, the sodden reed boat moved toward Barbados. The steering grew ever more difficult with the

added weight of tons of absorbed water. As it leaned in the wind, one side of the boat was pressed a foot under water. Sharks began accompanying the boat, making Georges' underwater inspections impossible. Thor was concerned that something might put so great a strain on weary *Ra II* that she might not make it. But men as well as the sea can be stubborn. And people stubborn together can do great things.

On Sunday, July 12, 1970, *Ra II* was on a hard reach to Barbados, when at nine in the morning a light plane buzzed in close. Eight pairs of eyes eagerly scanned the sky. Greetings crackled over the radio. There remained only thirty miles to go. The suspense of being *almost* there gripped the men.

By noon there was so much water on deck that the boxes on which the mattresses lay were floating. Norman climbed to the masthead to search the horizon. An hour later he shouted, "Land ho! Land ho!" The chorus swelled beneath him as the crew took up the chant. Madani and Kei strained for their first sight of the American islands. Santiago yelled "Olé!" Georges blew raucous blasts on the foghorn. Fifty-seven days at sea were nearly over.

Messages of congratulation from all over the world poured in on their radio. Planes and boats rushed to greet the heroic travelers sailing under the flag of the United Nations. Newsmen had gathered to meet them. Thor's wife and Norman's were on their way out to see them.

Carlo, jubilant and bursting with pride, uncorked a jar of their precious water and poured it over Yuri, Norman, and himself. There were tears of joy in the eyes of Thor Heyerdahl's men as they reached the end of the journey that had been called impossible. They cheered their great captain and each other. Eight men from eight nations, in a boat that might have sailed forty centuries before. They had sailed across the wide and salt Atlantic in a paper boat.

THOR HEYERDAHL